SOAR to the STRATOSPHERE

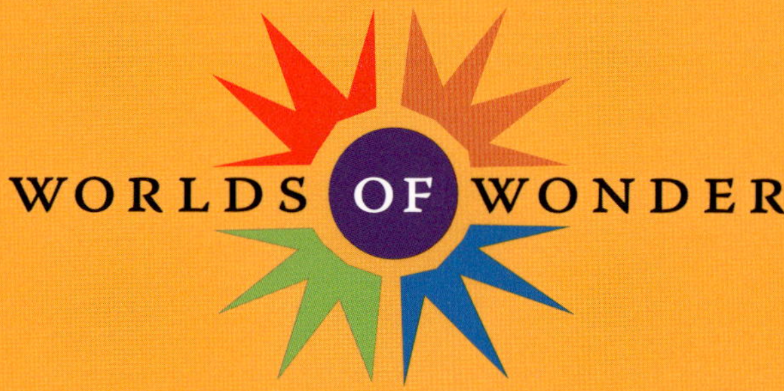

Barbara Guth Worlds of Wonder Science Series for Young Readers

This series explores a variety of scientific subjects to make them comprehensible and engaging for middle school–age readers. It seeks to convey the thrill of science and to inspire further inquiry into the wonders of scientific research and discovery. The series also aims to provide adults, particularly parents and grandparents, with accessible and stimulating books they can share with children.

Also available in the Barbara Guth Worlds of Wonder Science Series for Young Readers:

UFOhs! Mysteries in the Sky by Deborah Blumenthal and Ralph Blumenthal
The Raptors of North America: A Coloring Book of Eagles, Hawks, Falcons, and Owls by Anne Price
The Science of Soccer: A Bouncing Ball and a Banana Kick by John Taylor
Southwest Aquatic Habitats: On the Trail of Fish in a Desert by Daniel Shaw
Wonders of Nuclear Fusion: Creating an Ultimate Energy Source by Neal Singer
Eco-tracking: On the Trail of Habitat Change by Daniel Shaw
Cell Phone Science: What Happens When You Call and Why by Michele Sequeira and Michael Westphal
Powering the Future: New Energy Technologies by Eva Thaddeus
What Are Global Warming and Climate Change? Answers for Young Readers by Chuck McCutcheon
The Tree Rings' Tale: Understanding Our Changing Climate by John Fleck

Soar to the Stratosphere

Auguste Piccard's Incredible Balloon Flight to Dizzying Heights

Thomas Paone

Illustrated by Diane Kidd

University of New Mexico Press
Published in association with the Smithsonian Institution
Albuquerque

TO HENRY AND EMMA, FOR PROVIDING THE GIGGLES THAT INSPIRED THIS WHOLE PROJECT. AND TO AMANDA, WHO SUPPORTED THIS DREAM FROM START TO FINISH.

—THOMAS PAONE

TO MY DEAR FAMILY, FRIENDS, STORYTIME KIDDOS, AND EARLY CHILDHOOD EDUCATION VOLUNTEERS. KEEP REACHING FOR THE STARS.

—DIANE KIDD

Have you ever looked up at the sky

And wished to travel way up high?

Beyond the clouds, beneath the stars—
What might you see from heights so far?

One scientist had daring plans
For venturing above the land.

Auguste Piccard wanted to go
Up high to learn all he could know
About the things found in that place—
Like cosmic rays from outer space!

But how would Piccard reach such heights?
He'd need a special type of flight.
Not plane, nor kite—nor craft to the moon;

This trip called for a **GIANT** balloon!
He built a structure, six feet tall
Shaped like a giant basketball.

And with it tied to the balloon,
He'd surely reach the heavens soon.
In fact, this "gondola" would soar
Higher than anyone before!

mesosphere

stratosphere

Troposphere

EARTH

He'd travel up to where it's clear:
A region called the stratosphere.

But Piccard could not go alone.
He needed help to reach this zone!
Paul Kipfer, too, would join the flight.
Together, they could reach new heights!

But what to wear
in case of bumps?
To make it back
without new
lumps?
Not crown, nor cap,
nor armadillo!
Just some baskets
and soft pillows.

Ready now, they waved goodbye.
The pair set off into the sky.

Higher they went, then higher more.
Higher, higher did they soar!

Up they went, and up again
'Til they were higher even than

Two tall giraffes in stovepipe hats
Or even furry, flying bats!

Higher than mountains topped with goats—

So high, in fact, they wore thick coats.

50,000 feet!

Flying high was sometimes scary;
But they pushed on! They didn't tarry.
They went so high that they soon beat
A record: fifty thousand feet!

They studied air and cosmic rays.
The journey took almost all day!

At last they landed on thick ice:
A glacier in the mountain heights.

Then they returned home, to much delight,
Back from their daring, airy flight!

This gutsy journey way up there
Led to new facts about the air.
And others soon would reach heights greater:
Thanks to Piccard, more trips came later.

Piccard's brave flight kicked off a race
To fly higher still . . .

and one day to space!

The True Story of an Incredible Flight

Can you imagine soaring high into the stratosphere? Auguste Piccard did—in fact, this book describes a totally true tale!

A scientist named Auguste Piccard dreamed of flying higher than anyone had ever successfully flown before. He wanted to learn new things about the sky way up high. To do this, Piccard had to work hard to invent special tools that would help him fly to great heights . . . and return to the ground safely. The scientist used his tools to study the air in the area of the sky named the stratosphere. This helped Piccard learn new things about an area that few people had ever gone to before.

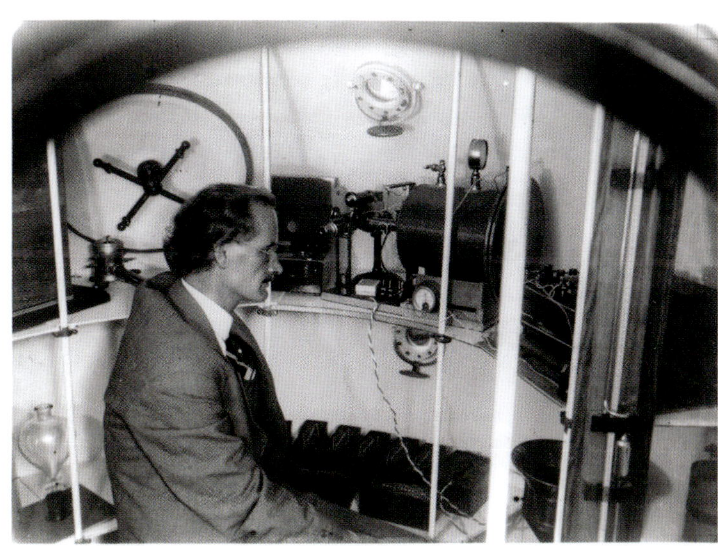

Dr. Auguste Piccard sits in the gondola of his first stratospheric exploration balloon (FNRS) in 1931.

EARTH'S ATMOSPHERE

The Earth is surrounded by something called the **atmosphere**. The atmosphere is made up of different layers of gases. It lets us breathe and live safely on the Earth. The Earth's atmosphere is made up of five layers: the troposphere, the stratosphere, the mesosphere, the thermosphere, and the exosphere.

Stratosphere: The second layer of Earth's atmosphere

A SUPERB SCIENTIST

Auguste Piccard was born in the country of Switzerland in 1884. He was interested in learning about the world, and he worked hard to become a scientist. In the 1930s, Piccard wanted to travel higher than anyone had before. Until then, people had traveled up to the atmosphere's first layer, the troposphere. But no one had successfully been to the stratosphere and returned safely!

Piccard wanted to journey to the stratosphere. There, he wanted to study something called cosmic rays. Cosmic rays are teeny, tiny pieces of energy, known as particles, that come from outer space! They are often blocked by the atmosphere, so Piccard wanted to go up as high as possible to study them better. Piccard wanted to learn more about these cosmic rays. He thought they might help scientists understand more about outer space and the universe.

Portrait photograph of balloonist Auguste Piccard.

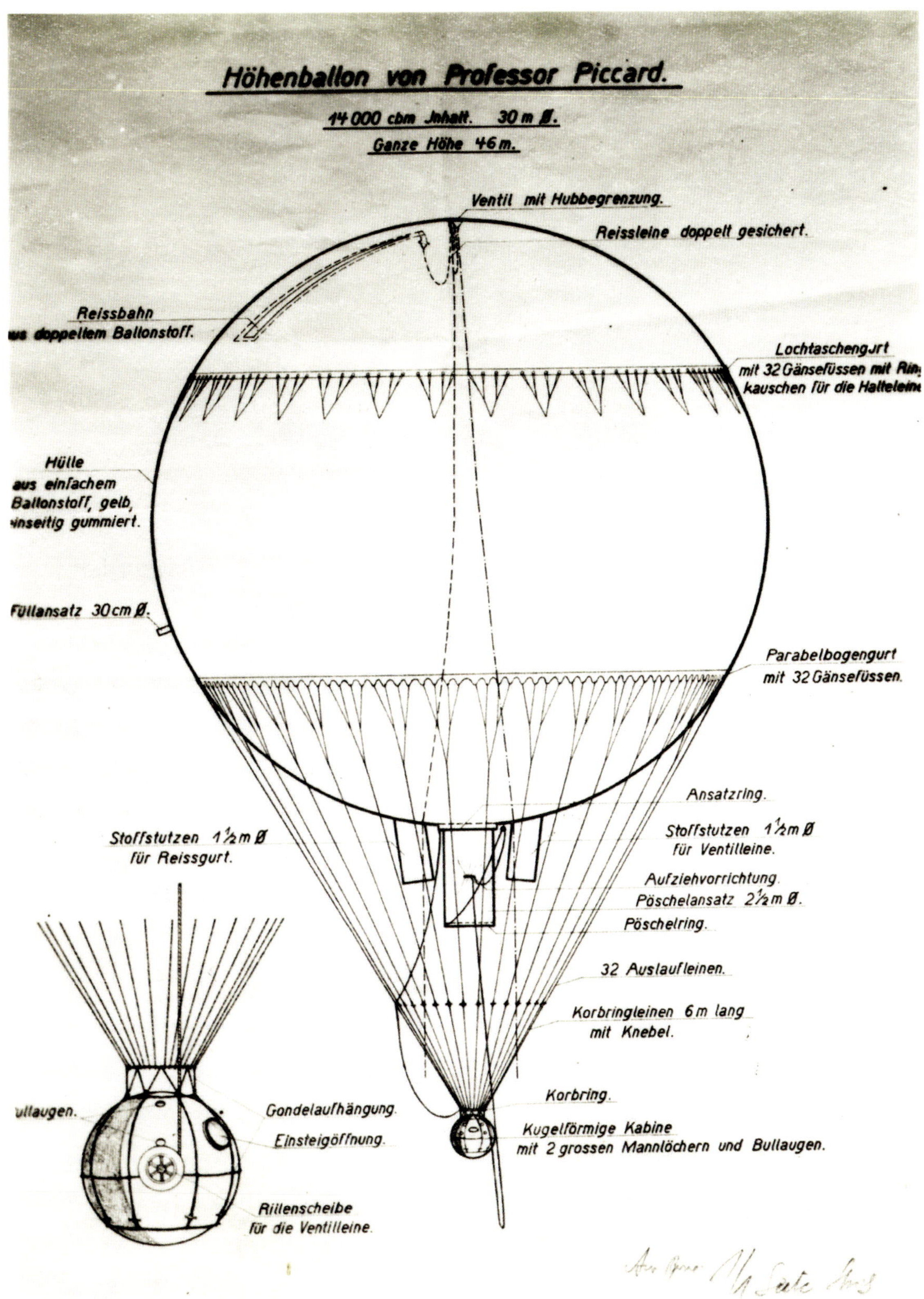

Drawing of Auguste Piccard's high-altitude balloon FNRS I, with details of the pressurized gondola (cabin) at lower right.

Chart showing the altitude flights of various persons attempting to break the world record before Piccard.

FLYING HIGH WITH GAS

It was not easy to get to the stratosphere in the 1930s. At the time, few airplanes could travel as high as the stratosphere because it was too cold and it was hard to breathe that high above the ground. Some planes had open cockpits, meaning pilots were exposed to cold temperatures and low oxygen levels at those heights. Even enclosed planes were not pressurized, meaning they were often very cold and uncomfortable when flying up high.

But Piccard discovered a way to fly really high! He had the idea to make a special flying machine. To do this,

Two men with the pressurized gondola for the balloon FRNS I suspended inside a workshop.

Piccard built a metal ball, called a gondola, to use as a container for himself and his scientific equipment. He attached the gondola to a very large gas balloon. Piccard pressurized this gondola, making it comfortable to breathe and work in at great heights.

Today, you might have seen hot air balloons high in the sky. Hot air balloons work by using fuel to operate a burner that heats the air in a balloon and keeps it warm as the balloon flies. Hot air rises, pulling the balloon up! But Auguste Piccard could not use a hot

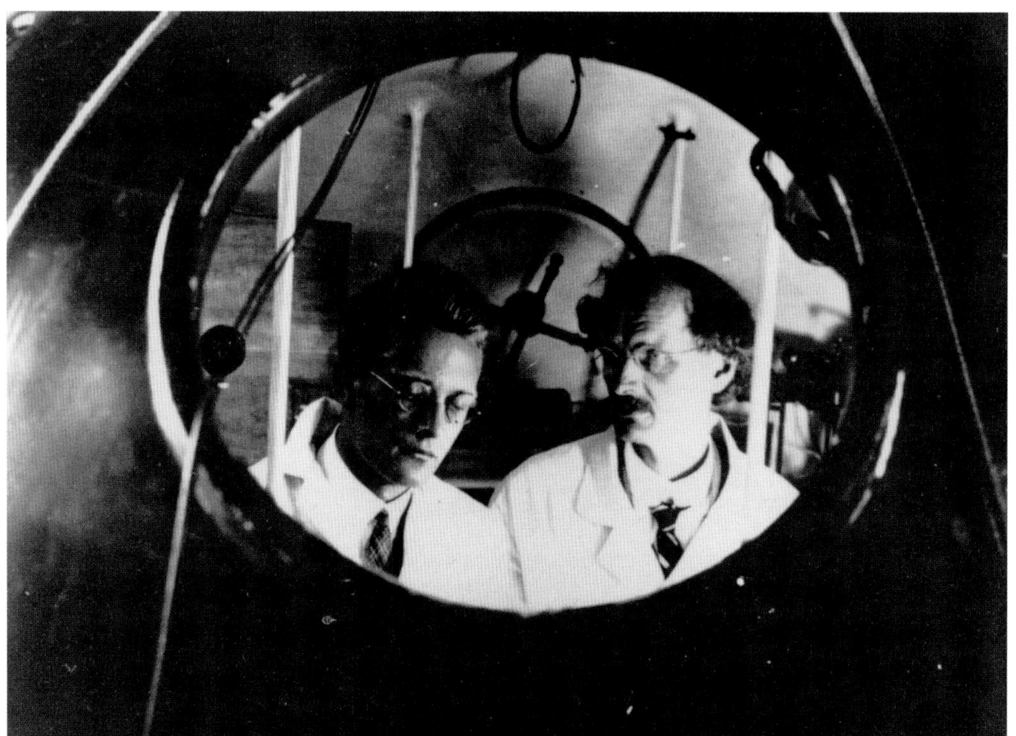

Paul Kipfer (*left*) and Auguste Piccard (*right*) inside the FNRS I gondola, circa 1931. It was named after the Belgian fund for scientific research, Fonds National de la Recherche Scientifique.

air balloon to make his flight to the stratosphere. The air is very cold at high altitudes, and the hot air balloon burners used today were not yet invented. Although hot air balloons were some of the first ever used, they could not keep the air hot as they flew higher and higher into the atmosphere. Piccard had to use a gas balloon instead.

This balloon was filled with a lifting gas called hydrogen. This gas is lighter than the air we breathe, and it allows the balloon to rise up into the air. Piccard had to make a very large balloon to hold lots of gas that could support the gondola, tools, and people for the flight.

Paul Kipfer (*left*) and Auguste Piccard (*right*) pose wearing crash helmets, circa 1930.

LIFTOFF!

On May 27, 1931, Auguste Piccard and his assistant Paul Kipfer set off in the gondola, bringing tools along with them for taking measurements. They traveled higher than 50,000 feet—higher than anyone had ever flown! There, they were able to observe the world through windows, or portholes, in the gondola, and they were able to collect some information on cosmic rays outside in the atmosphere.

The flight was sometimes dangerous, but Piccard and Kipfer were able to return

UNDER PRESSURE

Pressure is the force of one object pushing against another. You may not notice it, but the atmosphere puts pressure on you! When people travel out of the atmosphere, there is not enough pressure for them to be safe or comfortable.

Pressurize: To keep the pressure in a container at a certain level

safely to the ground. The first flight encountered some problems. To land, Piccard normally would let out some gas from the balloon, allowing it to slowly lower. But the rope to the valve that released the gas broke! Instead, they had to wait until the gas in the balloon cooled enough for them to land back on the ground. Because of this, only one measurement was made to test for cosmic rays. Piccard made a second flight on August 18, 1932, with his assistant Max Cosyns, and collected much more cosmic ray data.

The success of these flights encouraged other teams to fly even higher in their own balloons all over the world.

FLYING HIGH TODAY

We can fly much higher into the atmosphere today than Auguste Piccard was able to do in the 1930s. On October 14, 2012, Felix Baumgartner flew to over 120,000 feet in a specially designed capsule, much like Auguste Piccard. He decided to return to Earth by parachute, however, instead of landing in the gondola! On October 24, 2014, Alan Eustace flew to over 135,000 feet when he attached a gas balloon to his specially designed spacesuit. He released the balloon and fell back to Earth before releasing a parachute that let him land safely. These flights continue to inspire us to go higher and higher!

Make Your
Own Balloon Adventure

1.
Draw Balloon shape
2.
CUT OUT
3.
paper Balloon
7.
Tape
attach paper Balloon to yarn with tape
6
Tie the yarn To Basket corners

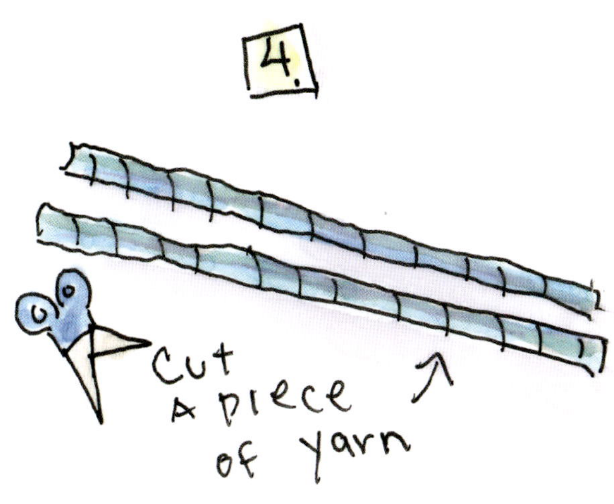
4.
Cut
a piece
of yarn

5
empty
a fruit
Basket

8.
Add
a
Toy

9.
Or
use
a
RUBBer
Balloon
10
Have fun!

Acknowledgments

Book projects like this require the work of so many people to make a random thought into a real book. We owe a great deal of gratitude to all those who helped make this a reality. Dr. Tom Crouch and Dr. David DeVorkin offered expertise and advice to ensure historical accuracy could be snuck into this fun story where possible. Jill Corcoran and Paige Towler kept this project alive and helped improve the manuscript through several iterations.

Printed in the United States of America

ISBN 978-0-8263-6975-8 (cloth)
ISBN 978-0-8263-6976-5 (ePub)

Library of Congress Control Number: 2026932171

Founded in 1889, the University of New Mexico sits on the traditional homelands of the Pueblo of Sandia. The original peoples of New Mexico—Pueblo, Navajo, and Apache—since time immemorial have deep connections to the land and have made significant contributions to the broader community statewide. We honor the land itself and those who remain stewards of this land throughout the generations and also acknowledge our committed relationship to Indigenous peoples. We gratefully recognize our history.

The University of New Mexico Press recognizes the contributions and assistance of the following staff at Smithsonian Enterprises:

Paige Towler, Editorial Lead
Jill Corcoran, Senior Director, Licensed Publishing
Brigid Ferraro, Vice President of New Business and Licensing
Carol LeBlanc, President

Cover art by Diane Kidd
Designed by Felicia Cedillos
Composed in Alegreya Sans